Brown v. Board of Education (1954)

By MARK E. DUDLEY

TWENTY-FIRST CENTURY
BOOKS
A Division of
Henry Holt and Company

New York

For my father, Edward Elias Dudley,
who showed me what it means to be fair.

Twenty-First Century Books
A Division of Henry Holt and Company, Inc.
115 West 18th Street
New York, NY 10011

Henry Holt ® and colophon are trademarks of
Henry Holt and Company, Inc.
Publishers since 1866

Library of Congress Cataloging-in-Publication Data
Dudley, Mark E.
Brown v. Board of Education (1954) : school desegregation / Mark E. Dudley.—1st ed.
p. cm.—(Supreme Court decisions)
Includes bibliographical references and index.
1. Brown, Oliver, 1918- —Trials, litigation, etc.—Juvenile literature.
2. Topeka (Kan.). Board of Education—Trials, litigation, etc.—Juvenile literature.
3. Segregation in education—Law and legislation—United States—Juvenile literature.
I. Title. II. Title: Brown versus Board of Education. III. Series: Supreme Court decisions (New York, N.Y.)
KF228.B76D83 1994b   344.73'0798—dc20   94-21862
[347.304798]   CIP AC

Photo Credits
All photos provided by AP / Wide World Photos

Design
Tina Tarr-Emmons

Typesetting and Layout
Custom Communications

ISBN 0-8050-3657-1
First Edition 1994

Printed in Mexico
All first editions are printed on acid-free paper ∞.

10 9 8 7 6 5 4 3 2 1

Contents

An End and a Beginning

On May 17, 1954, the Supreme Court of the United States announced its unanimous decision that the segregation of public schools by law was unconstitutional and would no longer be allowed in this country.

The decision marked the culmination of five separate but related cases that were filed in the early 1950s by black families. In each case, black students and their parents were protesting state policies that allowed or required separate schools for white children and black children. In all but one of the cases, the schools for the black children were vastly inferior to those attended by white children. The black parents and their children said this situation was not right.

In the end, the Supreme Court agreed. Its historic decision marked both an end and a beginning. It ended more than a century of state-sanctioned discrimination against black students. It also was a milestone in the movement for equality between the two races that continues today.

CHAPTER ONE

Five Cases

*If there is no struggle, there is no
progress. Those who profess to favor
freedom, and yet deprecate agitation,
are men who want crops without
plowing up the ground.[1]*

— Frederick Douglass

The summer of 1950 was a happy time for eight-year-old
Linda Carol Brown. She enjoyed playing with her two younger sisters and the
other children in the Topeka, Kansas, neighborhood in which she lived. The
railroad tracks passed close to their house, and sometimes the switchman would
wave as the train roared by the three sisters. "Hi, boys!" he would yell. The girls
would giggle and yell back, "Hi, Mary!"[2]

As autumn approached, Linda's father, the Reverend Oliver Brown, took
her for a walk one day. They walked seven blocks to Sumner Elementary
School, a pretty, new building on a tree-lined street. Linda waited while her
father went in to talk with the principal. A few minutes later, the Reverend
Brown came out, and they returned home. Linda could tell that her father was
upset. She did not find out why for quite some time.

The U.S. Supreme Court building in Washington, D.C.

One hundred years before Linda Brown went walking with her father, Kansas was simmering with tension. As the new territory was being carved out of the midwestern frontier, different factions struggled for power. Some of the settlers planned to use slaves to work the fertile soil and help build a new life. This was the custom of their forefathers in the southern states.

Others, from the North, were abolitionists. They regarded slavery as an evil institution and wanted no part of it in their new land. The dispute soon turned into violence, and the seeds of the Civil War were sown. A century later, the descendants of the slaves and freedmen who had settled the region still carried the stigma of the past.

The Reverend Brown was angry that summer day because the principal of Sumner had turned down his request to register Linda for classes that fall. Sumner Elementary was open to white children only. Topeka was one of several cities in Kansas where elementary schools were segregated. Blacks, Native Americans, and other minorities were not allowed to attend classes with white children. In 17 states, segregation was mandatory. Three other states, along with the District of Columbia, permitted their local school boards to separate their pupils by race.

Most blacks in the city begrudgingly accepted the school policy. They did not want their children to be taunted by white hooligans yelling racial slurs. Like his neighbors, the Reverend Brown was not the sort of man to cause trouble. But he did not want his daughter to have to walk six blocks along the railroad tracks in order to catch the bus to the rundown black school. He knew Linda played amicably with the white children in the neighborhood, as well as with the Native American and Hispanic children who lived nearby.

The Browns were not the only ones who wanted school segregation to end. Some of the black families in Topeka sought the help of the National Association for the Advancement of Colored People (NAACP). They tried appealing to the

Linda Brown in 1952

school board, but the authorities were obstinate. The board would not change its policy until the law itself was changed.

Convincing the Kansas legislature to desegregate the schools was an unlikely prospect. Legislators rarely upset the status quo unless there were votes at stake. Few blacks were allowed to vote in the South in those days. Many whites were sympathetic, but not enough to make a difference on Election Day. The best recourse, it seemed to the opponents of school segregation, was the courts.

Before going to court, the school segregation opponents wanted to find a strong, secure person to head the list of those filing the complaint. They realized that that person—the lead plaintiff—would be the target of severe criticism and perhaps even violence from those who supported school segregation. A school desegregation case would attract a great deal of publicity. Other people who had filed similar cases had lost their jobs and been labeled as troublemakers.

The NAACP decided that Oliver Brown's family was the best candidate. In addition to serving as a minister, the Reverend Brown had a union job—as a welder at the railroad—and likely would not be fired. He was a veteran and an assistant pastor at a conservative, respectable church. He was not a member of the NAACP and not likely to be viewed as an agitator.

The Reverend Brown was tired of being treated as a second-class citizen. He thought of his young daughter. "She seems very apt," he said. "I want her to have something more to look forward to than washing dishes."[3]

Brown agreed to head the list of plaintiffs protesting Topeka's segregated schools. Suit was filed in the United States District Court for the District of Kansas on February 28, 1951, as *Brown v. Board of Education of Topeka*. The battle had begun.

Other Cases Join the Fight

Meanwhile, the struggle for equality continued elsewhere. Wilmington was probably the most tolerant community in Delaware in 1951. But it was still inclined toward racial prejudice. All public schools, hospitals, restaurants, hotels, movie theaters, and even the National Guard segregated blacks from whites. Howard High School, where black students were assigned, was located in a seedy section of the downtown area. It was surrounded by factories, warehouses, and rundown tenements. For vocational training, the students had to walk nine blocks to a decrepit annex.

Nine miles north of the city, in suburban Claymont, Ethel Belton wondered why her children had to be bused for 50 minutes each way to Howard High every weekday. There was a new school right in Claymont—for whites only. Besides the convenient location and the better facilities, the Claymont school had many courses that Howard did not. Claymont students were offered Spanish, trigonometry, and economics, as well as a driver-education program and a student newspaper.

Fed up, Belton and seven other black parents went to see Louis Redding at his office in Wilmington. Redding had made a name for himself by becoming the first black lawyer in Delaware in 1929. The year before the Claymont parents visited him, Redding and Jack Greenberg, a lawyer for the NAACP, had successfully argued an important case before the state Chancery Court. The court had ordered blacks admitted to the University of Delaware for the first time. Perhaps now the time was ripe to extend this new freedom to high-school students.

Redding advised the parents to ask the state board of education to admit their children to the local white high school. As expected, they were turned down. Redding filed suit against the board in Chancery Court. The case became known as *Belton v. Gebhart*. Gebhart referred to Francis B. Gebhart, a member of the board. Because his name came first in an alphabetical list of the board members, the case was named after him.

Prince Edward County Blacks Seek Better Schools

In Prince Edward County, Virginia, the situation was far worse than in Topeka or Wilmington. Moton High School in Farmville, reserved for black students, was severely overcrowded. Several outbuildings that were little better than tar-paper shacks had been erected for classes that would not fit into the main school building. They were heated only by woodstoves and had no indoor toilets. The school's buses and other equipment, which had been discarded from the white schools, were often in poor repair.

Barbara Rose Johns was on the student council and traveled to other schools as a member of the drama club and chorus. She saw that the white schools in the area were far better than her own. In the autumn of 1950, she convinced the student council to ask the school board for better facilities for black students. The board told the students that a bond issue would have to be passed by the voters to build a new school.

For the next six months, nothing was done. Barbara decided that the students would have to take more direct action. At the end of April, a school assembly was announced, and the students and faculty gathered in the auditorium. Instead of the principal, Barbara Johns was at the rostrum. She asked the teachers to leave, and announced that she and her supporters were organizing a strike. She believed the only way to ensure better facilities for blacks would be for whites and blacks to attend the same schools.

For the next two weeks, the students picketed outside the school or stayed at their desks with closed books. Meanwhile, the student strike committee contacted the NAACP for help.

Oliver W. Hill, a Richmond attorney, agreed to meet with the students. The NAACP was looking for test cases with which to pursue the segregation issue. He could think of better places to start with than Prince Edward County, though. Racial prejudice ran deep in the small rural towns. It would be better to begin such cases in the more cosmopolitan cities. There, judges would be more sympathetic, and there would be less chance of a violent reaction against the plaintiffs.

But after meeting with Barbara Johns and her friends, he was impressed by their motivation and organization. He agreed to take their case if they could convince their parents to back them. That night, more than a thousand black supporters filled the auditorium of Moton High.

One month later, suit was filed in the federal court in Richmond in the name of Dorothy E. Davis, 14-year-old daughter of a local farmer. The suit was on behalf of 117 Moton students asking for an end to school segregation in Virginia. *Davis v. County School Board of Prince Edward County* began its slow journey through the courts.

Washington, D.C., Protesters Join the Fray

In 1950, Washington, D.C., had perhaps the worse slums in the country. The years since World War II had brought a population boom, and the shortage of affordable housing caused severe overcrowding in the black sections. Black schools were old, shabby, and ill-equipped. They often ran double and triple sessions to accommodate all the students.

In contrast, the white schools were half empty, the result of "white flight." Whites with better jobs had escaped from the poverty of their neighbors. They moved out of Washington into the new suburbs springing up on the outskirts of the city.

Gardner Bishop was a barber in one of the poorer sections of town. He did not think much of the NAACP lawyers with their fancy clothes and language. He did not like the way they catered to the black middle class who looked down their noses at their poorer brethren. But he needed help.

In 1949, Bishop had organized a student strike at Browne Junior High to protest the poor facilities. The NAACP was supporting the local PTA in its suit against the board of education over the same issue. The strike lasted two months. It won more sympathy in the white press than the lawsuit but made little headway in achieving any real progress.

Bishop finally visited an NAACP meeting featuring the renowned civil rights lawyer Charles Houston. After the meeting, Bishop asked Houston to support his cause. Houston had had little contact with the black underclass but was impressed with the man's desire to help the disadvantaged children of the nation's capital. Houston asked how much money Bishop's group had saved. Their meager treasury amounted to $14. "Well, you've got yourself a lawyer,"[4] Houston told him.

Bishop agreed to call off the student strike. In return, Houston said he would launch a series of suits in the Washington courts asking for equal treatment of black and white students. Bishop's group hoped they could force the district school board to build schools for the blacks that would be truly equal to those of the whites.

The next few months went badly. The Court of Appeals for the District of Columbia dismissed the PTA suit. Then Houston fell ill. From his deathbed, Houston told Bishop to contact James Madison Nabrit, Jr., another NAACP lawyer, to continue work on the suits.

Bishop visited Nabrit and explained the situation to him. Nabrit turned him down, saying that such suits were a waste of time and effort. Even if they won, he said, they would just have to turn around and file suit again for the next school and prove their case all over again. However, Nabrit told Bishop that if he agreed to sue on the basis that segregation of the schools was in itself unjust, the ruling would have much broader application. Bishop agreed.

In early September of 1950, Gardner Bishop led a group of 11 black children and concerned parents to John Philip Sousa Junior High School to

Spottswood Thomas Bolling, Jr., a 14-year-old freshman at Spingarn High School in Washington, D.C., awaits the outcome of the Supreme Court case on school desegregation. He was one of the plaintiffs in the case.

enroll for the school year. Twelve-year-old Spottswood Thomas Bolling, Jr., and his brother Wanamaker were accompanied by their mother. She did not like the poor conditions in Shaw Junior High, Spottswood's current school. There the science lab equipment included only a single Bunsen burner and a bowl of goldfish.

The principal was sympathetic but said she was not authorized to enroll them—Sousa was a white school. Next they visited the superintendent of schools, where they got the same answer. Then they approached the board of education. The president of the board, C. Melvin Sharpe, told them Congress had made its wishes quite clear on the matter. The legislators had appropriated funds for two sets of schools—one white and one black. Bishop and his young plaintiffs had gone through the motions. Next stop was the U.S. District Court, where suit was filed in early 1951 as *Bolling v. Sharpe*.

South Carolina Schools Among the Worst

Of the five desegregation suits that were eventually brought before the Supreme Court, conditions were clearly the worst in the case from Clarendon County, South Carolina. Schools for the 6,500 black students in the county were assessed at less than a third of the value of the schools for the 2,300 white students. County spending for blacks was less than a quarter of that for whites. The school board provided only for the black teachers' salaries—at two-thirds the rate for white teachers—and not for supplies or building maintenance.

In Summerton, a small agricultural town where sharecroppers still worked the land, there were no school buses for blacks. Only a few black children were willing to walk the nine miles to the high school. They watched with envy as the white students roared by them in their new buses. Even the younger children had to row across flooded roads at times to reach the school. There they studied in miserable little shacks.

Compulsory school attendance was not enforced for the blacks. They were needed in the white farmers' fields at planting and harvest time.

The Reverend Joseph Albert DeLaine believed he had to do something for the children. He circulated a petition among the black farmers asking for public funding for a school bus. The minister thought this would be a safe place to start.

DeLaine and a group of friends took their petition to the superintendent of schools, the Reverend L. B. McCord, but he rejected it. He told DeLaine that it would be unfair to the whites in the district, who paid most of the taxes, to support a black school bus.

A lawsuit was filed next with the help of the NAACP's Legal Defense Fund head, Thurgood Marshall. However, the suit was dismissed due to confusion over the location of the plaintiff's house in the school district. The principal of the black high school was fired soon after, suspected of encouraging the suit. Levi Pearson, the plaintiff, chosen because he owned his own farm, found that none of the local banks would lend him money for seeds or fertilizer. His neighbors scraped together some money for him, but when harvest time came, none of the white farmers would rent him a harvester. His crops rotted in the field.

A second petition and lawsuit was filed in Harry Briggs's name against Roderick W. Elliot, chairman of the school district. In retaliation, Briggs was fired from the job he had held at the local service station for the last 14 years. His wife, a maid, was let go, too. The local whites in power clearly wanted to discourage anyone from bringing in outside agitators.

By the time the case, *Briggs v. Elliot*, had made its way to the Supreme Court, the school board had fired the Reverend DeLaine from his teaching job of ten years. His wife, two sisters, his niece, and several other blacks who signed the petition also lost their jobs. DeLaine's house was burned while the firefighters stood and watched without helping. Mobs stoned the church where DeLaine preached and later burned it to the ground.

Town leaders even arrested Harry Briggs's cow when it got loose one night and stepped on a white man's grave. All blacks suffered because they had asked for a school bus. But the Reverend DeLaine's faith was never shaken. It had been a long time coming, but he knew that, someday, justice would be theirs.

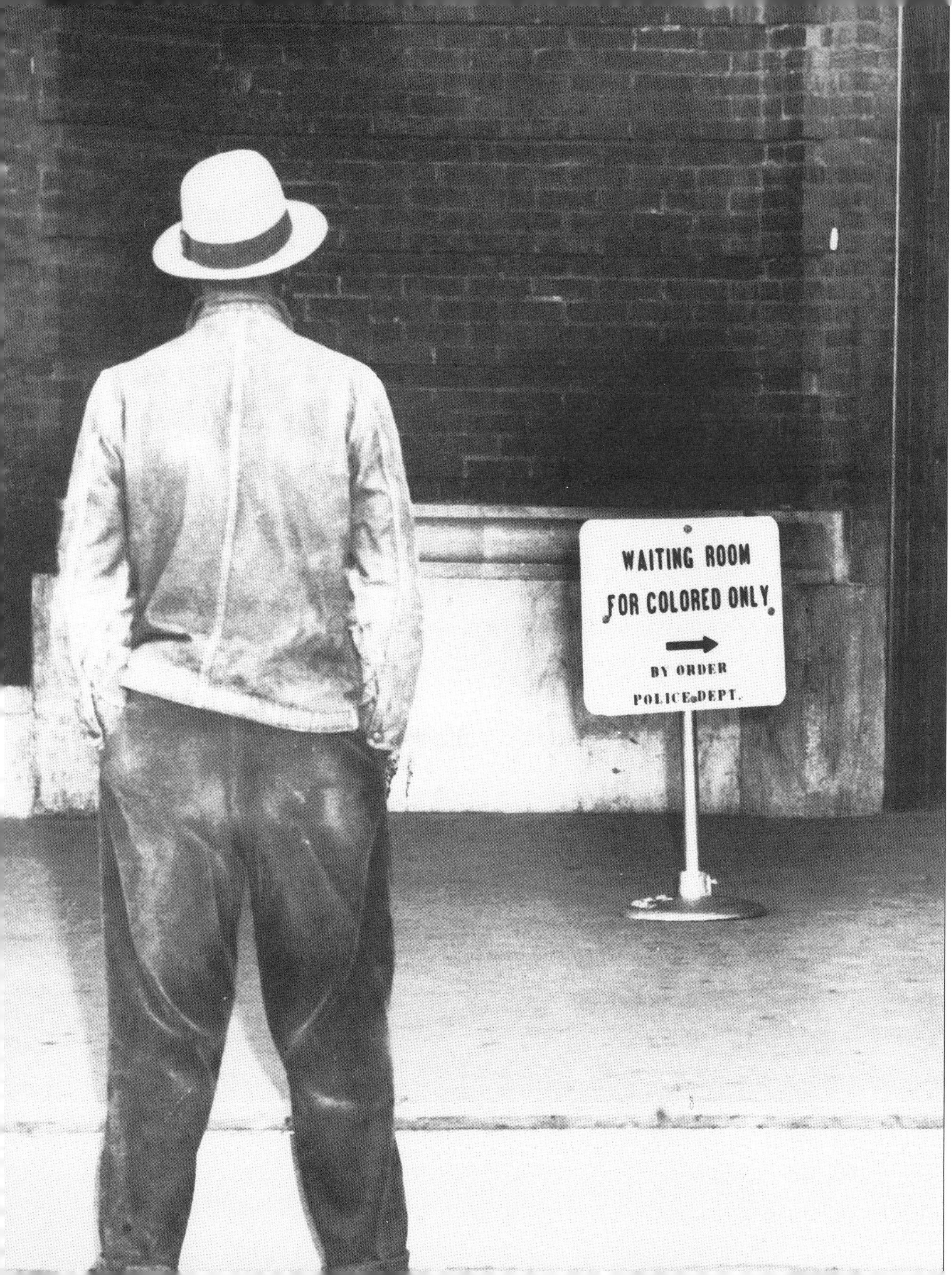
WAITING ROOM
FOR COLORED ONLY
BY ORDER
POLICE DEPT.

CHAPTER TWO

Separate and Unequal

*Our Constitution is color-blind, and
neither knows nor tolerates classes
among its citizens. In respect of civil
rights, all citizens are equal before
the law.*[1]

— **Justice John Marshall Harlan
in his dissent in *Plessy v. Ferguson***

The school desegregation cases had their roots in the
social upheaval following the Civil War. After the Confederate forces were
defeated, the federal government controlled the southern states. This period,
from 1865 to 1877, was called the Reconstruction.

During this time, the government was controlled by two factions. The
Radicals did not want the former leaders of the South to have any role in
reshaping their state governments. They wanted to provide land grants and
other economic help to the freed slaves. The Moderates' only concern was to put
the federal government back in control of the state governments. They would
do no more than guarantee basic civil rights to the blacks.

The Thirteenth Amendment, approved in 1865 before General Robert E.

A sign at a Jackson, Mississippi, bus station tells the story of a segregated nation.

Lee's surrender, had freed the slaves. But it did little else to improve their status. Southern legislatures hurried to adopt the so-called Black Codes. These were laws designed to keep blacks powerless, though technically free.

Blacks without jobs were assigned "guardians" to provide work and shelter—without pay. The guardians were often their former masters. Blacks were not allowed to vote, carry arms, testify against whites, or move about freely. The most enduring legacy of this period were the "Jim Crow" laws. Jim Crow was a nickname whites had used to describe blacks since the turn of the century. It was popularized by blackface entertainer Thomas "Daddy" Rice, who sang an old slave song:

> Wheel about and turn about and do just so.
> Every time I wheel about I jump like Jim Crow.[2]

Later, Jim Crow came to refer to the laws that segregated blacks from whites in public places and at public functions.

The Radicals hurried to help the oppressed blacks. They set up the Freedman's Bureau to help provide food, shelter, job assistance, and education for blacks and whites displaced by the war. Within two decades of Lincoln's election, the percentage of black children in school increased from 2 percent to more than 30 percent. (The number of whites attending school remained fairly constant at 60 percent.)

Congress passed a civil rights bill in 1866 granting citizenship to blacks. The bill guaranteed the same civil rights to all males born in the United States.

The Fourteenth Amendment Is Ratified

Then, in 1868, the states ratified the Fourteenth Amendment to the Constitution. This amendment would later be used as a basis for striking down school segregation. The amendment is divided into five sections. Those seeking desegregation in the schools used the equal protection clause in the first section of the amendment. The amendment's first section guarantees that: "no state shall make or enforce any law which shall abridge the privileges or immunities of citizens of the United States; nor shall any state deprive any person of life, liberty, or property, without due process of law; nor deny to any person within its jurisdiction the equal protection of the laws."

Radicals Gain Power

The Radicals soon gained more power. Congress provided for black men to become voters in 1867. Blacks were enthusiastic voters, electing many local black officials, and even two black U.S. senators. However, they gained little in the way of real power.

General Ulysses S. Grant was elected president in 1868 with the help of black voters. To retain power, the Republicans pushed through the Fifteenth Amendment in 1870. This amendment made voting by blacks a constitutional right.

The year 1875 was the high point for black rights in this era. The Civil Rights Act of 1875 prohibited discrimination due to race in public housing, transportation, theaters, and juries. It soon became clear, though, that the measure was intended only to buy votes from the blacks and abolitionists. Grant's administration only weakly enforced the act. As the passions of the war faded, blacks soon began losing ground.

A close presidential election in 1876 weakened the civil rights of blacks even further. The election hinged on the votes of three southern states. Though the popular vote went to Samuel J. Tilden, the Democratic candidate, the outcome depended on the electoral college. Twenty electoral votes were disputed. The decision lay in the hands of a Congress divided along party lines.

Ulysses S. Grant as president of the United States

A compromise was reached just two days before the inauguration. The southern votes would go to Republican Rutherford B. Hayes if the last federal troops were withdrawn from the southern states. The South was soon free to run its local affairs as it saw fit.

Throughout the South, blacks were prevented from voting through indirect means. Gerrymandering, redrawing voting district lines to benefit a specific group, ensured white majorities in local elections. Polls were set up far from black residential areas. Soon, discrimination took a more overt form. Blacks were required to pay expensive poll taxes before they could vote. They also had to pass literacy tests. White election officials decided who passed the tests.

These strategies were often intended to prevent poor whites from voting as well. The Populist party gained notice in the late 1880s as a coalition of blacks and poor whites. However, the Populists never grew strong enough to make any real inroads in the power structure.

Louisiana developed the most effective weapon against the Populists in 1898. The state's "grandfather clause" dropped literacy tests for would-be voters as long as their fathers or grandfathers were registered voters before 1867. That eliminated all illiterate blacks from the polls, since they had not won the right to vote until 1867.

The tactic was quite effective. A total of 130,000 blacks had been registered to vote in Louisiana in 1896. Two years after the clause took effect, that number dropped to 5,300. Poor whites, once brothers in arms, soon turned against blacks when threatened with losing their own right to vote.

Blacks also lost headway in the courts. A seemingly unrelated issue before the Supreme Court marked the beginning of the erosion of their rights. In the slaughterhouse cases, the Court ruled that Louisiana had the right to grant a monopoly franchise to a butchering firm. The result was that the firm would have exclusive control over business in a certain area. It would put other slaughterhouses out of business.

Rival slaughterhouses claimed that Louisiana had made a law that interfered with their privilege of earning a living. That action, they claimed, was a violation of the Fourteenth Amendment. But the Court ruled that the privileges and immunities clause of the amendment applied only to national rights. According to the Court, the clause gave citizens such rights as access to federal buildings and ports and voting in national elections.

The states seized on this reasoning to control local voting procedures. When a black man brought suit in Kentucky after being denied the right to vote in a local election, the Supreme Court, in *U.S. v. Reese*, declared that only the states could grant the right to vote in state and local elections.

The Fifteenth Amendment, passed six years earlier, proved to be ineffective as well in protecting black voters. The Court ruled it was up to the plaintiff to prove that he had been refused the vote only because he was black. Kentucky had no law denying the vote to blacks. White workers simply turned black men away at the poll, no reason given.

More ground was lost in the civil rights cases of 1883. Blacks throughout the nation were suing to prevent owners and managers of theaters, hotels, and the like from barring them from their facilities. In most places, this action was not a matter of the law but was left up to each business.

In these cases, the Supreme Court found the Civil Rights Act of 1875 to be unconstitutional. That act had been based on the Fourteenth Amendment, but the Court declared that the amendment applied only to government-run activities. According to the ruling, no law protected blacks from discrimination by private individuals. Jim Crow laws now were beyond the reach of the federal government and spread rapidly throughout the South.

The final nail was driven into the coffin of black rights with the Court's

Jim Crow laws kept blacks out of theaters, hotels, and other facilities. Here, George H. Guy, police chief in McComb, Mississippi, stands beside a sign at the local bus station that reserves a waiting room for whites only.

decision in *Plessy v. Ferguson* in 1896. New Orleans, at the end of the century, was perhaps the most liberal and cosmopolitan city in the South. The local populace was a mixture of English, French, Spanish, black, and Native American cultures.

People had little patience when the state legislature passed a law in 1890 titled "An Act to Promote the Comfort of Passengers," forbidding blacks to ride on white railroad cars. The railroads, balking at the expense of adding extra cars, were sympathetic to the blacks and did little to enforce the law. Even though the law was not enforced, blacks considered it insulting and decided to challenge it.

This was clearly not a case of discrimination by private individuals. Railroads running on interstate lines were under the control of the U.S. Congress. And plaintiffs would not have to prove that they were being discriminated against only because of their race. The law plainly stated that the railroads would provide "equal but separate accommodations for the white and colored races."[3]

Homer Adolph Plessy boarded the East Louisiana Railway in June of 1892 and sat down in the coach reserved for whites. As arranged, a conductor asked him to move. He refused, and a railway detective arrested him. Plessy was soon standing before Judge John H. Ferguson in the local court, where he was pronounced guilty.

The case was appealed and eventually ended up in the U.S. Supreme Court. The Court ruled against Plessy. He had argued that the Louisiana law violated the Fourteenth Amendment. Justice Henry Billings Brown, writing for the Court, found otherwise. The Fourteenth Amendment, he declared, while designed to force equality between the races, was not "intended to abolish distinctions based on color, or to enforce social, as distinguished from political, equality."[4]

In words boding ill for black schoolchildren of the next century, Justice Brown continued:

> [Segregated facilities] do not necessarily imply the inferiority of either race to the other, and have been generally, if not universally, recognized as within the competency of state legislatures in the exercise of their police power. The most common instance of this is connected with the establishment of separate schools for white and colored children.[5]

Justice John Marshall Harlan, however, dissented in strong words. His arguments would be echoed more than a half century later by civil rights lawyers arguing the school desegregation cases:

> The arbitrary separation of citizens, on the basis of race, while they are on a public highway, is a badge of servitude wholly inconsistent with the civil freedom and the equality before the law established by the constitution. It cannot be justified upon any legal grounds.[6]

The 19th century closed on a dismal note. Three years after *Plessy*, the Supreme Court declined to stop Richmond County, Georgia, from shutting down a black high school, while leaving the white school open. In *Cumming v. Richmond County Board of Education*, the Court said the schools were supported by state taxes and, hence, not a matter for federal courts.

In 1908, the *Berea College v. Kentucky* case allowed states to outlaw even private interracial schools. This blatantly discriminatory ruling led to widespread laws throughout the South requiring separation of the races in all aspects of life. Restaurants, saloons, and hotels turned blacks away at the door. Sporting events and plays were segregated. Signs were posted at rest rooms and water fountains designating the race they served. Even the courts provided separate Bibles for black witnesses to swear an oath. Jim Crow had come into its own.

As the 20th century began its course, the industrial revolution roared into the South. Factories had begun replacing mills decades before in the North. The largely agricultural South was only now broadening its economic base. The spread of the boll weevil in 1910 severely damaged the cotton crop, and plantation life became a thing of the past. Sharecroppers flocked to the cities, seeking a better life. There they found themselves competing for jobs with whites who had disdained fieldwork.

Competition soon led to conflict. The economy was still struggling as a result of the Civil War and could not support so many workers. Northern cities were even more inhospitable to blacks. There, European immigrants flooded the shores, more than filling the demand for unskilled labor.

As public opinion swung against blacks, the government turned a deaf ear to their plight. Woodrow Wilson's administration continued the trend toward separation of the races. The Post Office, the Department of the Treasury, and the Bureau of the Census were ordered to segregate. Black workers' desks were curtained off and cafeterias closed to them. Banks, insurance companies, and labor unions were allowed to discriminate with impunity. Lynchings and terrorism became common.

World War I brought some respite. European immigration stopped, and the war industry drew many southern blacks to northern cities. After the war ended, troops returning to the North found jobs scarce once again. White supremacists, who believed whites were better than blacks, fanned fears of intermarriage between races. They spread reports of black soldiers freely mingling with the grateful citizens of Europe, where racial discrimination was less common than in the United States. Race riots broke out in northern cities for the first time.

As the Depression strengthened its grip on the nation in the 1930s, blacks, already among the poorest, found conditions growing intolerable. More blacks were prevented from voting. The Supreme Court, in a series of cases, failed to stop southern states from excluding blacks from voting in primary elections. In the heavily Democratic South, the primary provided the decisive vote.

State officials had turned control of primaries over to the parties themselves. The Court ruled that the political parties were private organizations and, hence, beyond the jurisdiction of federal courts. Blacks were removed from the parties' membership rolls. People who had no vote received little attention from politicians whose main interest was their own reelection.

Into this climate of repression came a breath of fresh air. In 1933, Franklin Delano Roosevelt brought to the White House the best hope for blacks since Abraham Lincoln was president. For the first time, the door to the Oval Office was open to black leaders. Most departments had a section head or adviser to address black concerns. Roosevelt's New Deal legislation provided the first opportunity for federal help for much of the black population. More than 100,000 adult blacks learned to read and write as part of the Works Progress Administration programs. Twice that many found work in the Civilian Conservation Corps.

When the United States entered World War II, in 1941, literacy programs were stepped up. The sad condition of southern schools, in particular, became obvious as the draft slowly stripped the South of its young white men. The same legislators who had denied decent educations to blacks now complained that too many whites were being inducted into the service. Blacks were left behind after failing the military's literacy tests. The problem was made worse by the military's segregation policies. Whole units of blacks were found to be undereducated. Nevertheless, one million blacks served in the armed forces during the war.

On the homefront, two million blacks found work in the war plants. With the economy bustling like never before and 15 million men and women in the military, there was no lack of jobs. President Roosevelt issued an executive order that there would be no discrimination in defense hiring. Labor unions opened their doors to blacks. Government training programs provided new job skills and decent wages to people who had known nothing but poverty all their lives. At last, blacks began to feel as if they were participating in national affairs.

The world was changing. As the war ended, the new president, Harry S Truman, ordered the armed forces to desegregate. He began to abolish segregation in federal civil service positions. Blacks were appointed to high offices for the first time. Returning troops had seen a wide world where discrimination was uncommon. The GI Bill allowed blacks to attend college in record numbers. A booming economy had resulted in a large black middle class, and the NAACP's treasury grew.

Perhaps most important for the growing civil rights movement was the appointment of liberals to the Supreme Court by two Democratic administrations. It was time to push for desegregation where it mattered most—in the schools.

CHAPTER THREE

The Lower Courts

If we had not threatened to challenge the legality of the segregation system and if we do not continue the challenge to segregated schools, we will get the same thing we have been getting all these years—separate but never equal.[1]

—Thurgood Marshall

In the years before *Brown* came to court, some progress had been made in reversing segregation in higher education. To avoid admitting the few blacks applying to graduate schools, southern states typically sent them to northern schools. In 1935, Lloyd Lionel Gaines applied to the University of Missouri's law school. As expected, he was turned down because he was black. The state offered to send him to an out-of-state school. Though Missouri would pay the difference in the price of the tuition, Gaines would have to pay transportation costs himself. More importantly, he wanted to practice law in his home state, and the best place to study Missouri law was at the university.

Gaines brought suit against the registrar of the university, S. W. Canada.

The case made its way to the Supreme Court in 1938 as *Missouri ex rel. Gaines v. Canada*. In keeping with the "separate but equal" provision of *Plessy*, the Court ordered Missouri either to build a new law school for blacks or to admit Gaines. Gaines never pursued his education, but an important precedent was set.

Separate but Not Equal

Ada Lois Sipuel encountered a similar situation in 1948, when she applied to law school in Oklahoma. In this instance, Oklahoma was building a law school for blacks. Sipuel was told to wait. Thurgood Marshall argued before the Supreme Court that if white students were entitled to immediate admission, then so was his client. The Court concurred in *Sipuel v. Oklahoma State Board of Regents*, and the state was ordered to admit Sipuel.

Stubbornly, Oklahoma avoided admitting Sipuel to the white law school by creating one for her overnight by roping off a section of the state capitol building and providing three part-time instructors. Marshall returned to court to argue that such an arrangement could not provide an equal education. The court could offer no further relief, though, since the issue of equality had not been raised in the original suit. Marshall would soon have a chance to argue just such a point in two other cases.

Heman Marion Sweatt was a postman who wanted to become a lawyer. His application to the University of Texas at Austin in 1946 was rejected, again on racial grounds. Facing a lower court order, Texas tried a similar tactic to Oklahoma's. State authorities rented a few rooms, hired two lawyers to teach, and called it a law school. By the time Sweatt's case was appealed, the state, fearing court action, had improved their facility by adding trained faculty and a library.

Marshall argued before the Travis County Court that it was still impossible for Sweatt to receive an education equal to the white students'. As a law-school dean testified at the trial, " . . . it isn't enough to have a good professor. It is equally essential that there be a well-rounded, representative group of students in the classroom. . . ."[2] The students of the university agreed. Almost 2,000 supporters showed up at a rally to support Marshall's efforts. They even formed a new division of the NAACP, the only all-white branch at that time in the country.

Once again, the court ruled against the black plaintiff. It would take three years for *Sweatt v. Painter* to reach the U.S. Supreme Court. In the meantime, Marshall would handle a case that promised to define equality of education even further.

George W. McLaurin, like Ada Sipuel, had applied to the University of Oklahoma and been turned down. The District Court heard his case in August 1948 and ruled that he be admitted at once. Upon attending class, though, 68-year-old McLaurin discovered that he was forced to sit separated from the other students by a railing marked "Reserved For Colored." Disgusted white students tore down the barrier, but McLaurin was still assigned a seat apart from the other students. Here was a situation where the facilities and instruction were the same for black and white. The only inequity was in the segregation itself. Marshall had an opportunity to attack *Plessy* at its heart.

Both *McLaurin v. Oklahoma State Regents for Higher Education* and *Sweatt* were heard by the Supreme Court on the same day—April 3, 1950.

On June 5, the Court declared that the law school had created unequal conditions for Sweatt in "reputation of the faculty, experience of the administration, position and influence of the alumni, standing in the community, traditions, and prestige."[3] Part of a law school's job, the Court noted, was to help the student establish professional contacts. Doing so would be difficult in a smaller, all-black school. Sweatt was ordered admitted to the university.

The Court likewise found for the plaintiff in *McLaurin*. If the law school created for black students was not equal to that of white students, then segregated law schools would not be allowed, according to the Court. If facilities were integrated—open to both blacks and whites—there could be no restrictions or harassment, the Court ruled.

The NAACP had gone a long way this day toward achieving equality for blacks. But *Plessy* had not been struck down. The Court had ruled only that "separate but equal" meant truly equal. There were bigger battles to come. There was little public outcry against the few blacks being admitted to graduate schools. Integrating the lower grades would have a much greater impact on the nation.

Desegregating the Lower Schools

The first of the five school desegregation cases that would change history came before the District Court in 1950. The plaintiffs in *Bolling v. Sharpe* asked that schools in Washington, D.C., be desegregated on the grounds that segregation was unjust.

The citizens of Washington, D.C., were not covered by the Fourteenth Amendment. The amendment applied to states only. Therefore, James Nabrit, Jr., attorney for the plaintiff, decided to argue that segregation was a violation of the Fifth Amendment. The Fifth Amendment stated, "No person shall . . . be deprived of life, liberty, or property, without due process of law."[4]

Nabrit drew his argument from a 1923 Supreme Court case called *Meyer v. Nebraska*, involving the right of students to study German in public schools. The Court had written in its decision that the Fifth Amendment guaranteed the "right of the individual to acquire useful knowledge." and that this right was "not to be interfered with . . . by legislative action which is arbitrary."[5] James Nabrit, Jr., maintained that there was no reasonable basis for segregation of

34

Washington's schools. He claimed that the separation of white and black students was indeed arbitrary.

Furthermore, Nabrit argued, if Congress truly intended the capital's schools to remain segregated, it would have made the practice mandatory. Nabrit claimed it would have been illegal for Congress to require such a policy anyway, since Article 1 of the Constitution prohibited bills of attainder. A bill of attainder is a legislative action "which inflicts punishment without a judicial trial."[6]

The District Court did not buy Nabrit's reasoning. In April 1951, it ruled against Bolling and his fellow plaintiffs. Their only recourse would be a higher court. Nabrit readied an appeal while elsewhere the NAACP continued its struggle.

Defeat in District Court

A month after the *Bolling* decision, the second of the five desegregation cases was heard. NAACP attorneys Robert Carter and Thurgood Marshall asked the three-judge panel of the U.S. District Court in South Carolina to desegregate Clarendon County schools on behalf of Harry Briggs and the other plaintiffs. Judge John J. Parker presided.

The attorney for the state of South Carolina in the *Briggs* case was Robert Figg. He knew the NAACP lawyers would have little trouble proving the black and white school systems in the county were far from equal. He conceded as much at the beginning of the trial. Figg announced that the state legislature had approved new measures to address the inequity. He contended that the state should have time to correct past mistakes.

Marshall was surprised by the admission, but went on to document just how bad the situation really was. He doubted that, given the magnitude of the problem, South Carolina was really sincere about helping the blacks. It would take $40 million to bring black school buildings up to the level of the white schools. And, Marshall noted, there was more to education than just the physical condition of the structures.

Robert Carter then took up the argument. In the past, judicial decisions were governed strictly by existing law and precedent—that is, by what past courts had decided. Several years before, though, the NAACP had successfully used the results of tests and questionnaires to argue its case in *Shelley v. Kraemer*. The tests showed that discrimination in housing can cause psychological harm. Carter now used similar evidence to establish that segregation in the schools was unhealthy.

Figg, in his turn, relied on the "separate but equal" clause of the *Plessy* decision. The Fourteenth Amendment could not have been meant to apply to schools, he argued, or the same Congress would not have passed legislation establishing segregated schools in the nation's capital. Figg hinted darkly that, if forced to integrate, the state and local communities might cease to collect taxes for any public schools.

Three weeks later the court handed down its decision in the *Briggs* case. The plaintiffs' motion to desegregate was denied. The recent Supreme Court decisions in *Sweatt* and *McLaurin* did not apply, Judge Parker said. Unlike graduate school, public education at lower levels was required. According to the judge, the schools' job was to educate children, not to guarantee the reputation of the staff or help students establish professional contacts.

Brown Gets His Day in Court

Marshall had assumed that they would lose. It was a necessary step, he believed, on the road to the High Court. He hurried to complete preparations for the next test case. Oliver Brown was to have his day in court four days after the *Briggs* decision was announced. Robert Carter and Jack Greenberg began

Harry Briggs stands in front of the Scott's Branch School in Summerton, North Carolina, in 1979. In 1951 the U.S. District Court in South Carolina ruled against his bid to desegregate the schools.

arguing *Brown v. Board of Education* in Topeka June 25, 1951, before the United States District Court for Kansas.

The plaintiffs' attorneys knew it would be hard to convince the court that the Topeka school system was unequal for blacks and whites. Courses and buildings were largely the same for students of both races. Black students had to walk long distances past white schools to get to their own schools. However, some white students also walked many blocks every day, and Topeka provided buses for the blacks.

Mostly, the attorneys relied on testimony based on studies of human behavior. Expert witnesses told the court that when black children were set apart, they came to believe they were not smart enough to go to school with whites. A professor of psychology explained to the court, "If we din it into a person that he is incapable of learning, then he is less likely to be able to learn."[7] One final point was made: The black children would be spending their adult lives in a society that was 90 percent white. Could not it be considered an essential part of their education to learn to associate with their white peers?

Judge Walter Huxman spoke for a unanimous court five weeks later. Although clearly in sympathy with the plaintiffs, he found the schools to be substantially equal. The *McLaurin* and *Sweatt* decisions had been restricted by the Supreme Court to apply to graduate schools only. Although the decision was against the plaintiffs, Huxman attached a "Finding of Fact" to the opinion. It read in part:

> Segregation of white and colored children in
> public schools has a detrimental effect upon the
> colored children. The impact is greater when it
> has the sanction of the law; for the policy of
> separating the races is usually interpreted as

denoting the inferiority of the Negro group. A
sense of inferiority affects the motivation of a child
to learn.[8]

Years later, Judge Huxman recalled, "We were not in sympathy with the decision we rendered. If it were not for *Plessy v. Ferguson*, we surely would have found the law unconstitutional. But there was no way around it—the Supreme Court had to overrule itself."[9]

Segregation Creates Inequality

Late October brought the next case to court. Fortunately, *Belton v. Gebhart* would be argued before Judge Collins Seitz. He was the same judge who had ordered the University of Delaware desegregated the previous year. Redding and Greenberg followed the NAACP's usual tactic of relying on the expert testimony of social scientists to prove that segregation itself was discrimination. Then they documented inequalities in the school systems as a fallback position.

This time, the court heard evidence on the adverse effects of the long bus ride the plaintiffs had to undergo every day. A psychiatrist presented the results of tests on white and black children that showed both groups thought of segregation as punishment. Other witnesses testified that whites and blacks had the same intellectual abilities. The court heard that segregation often resulted in apathy or hostility among its victims.

Judge Seitz wanted to look at the schools himself. After inspecting the white students' beautiful Claymont School, Seitz found conditions at Howard High deplorable. In his opinion, delivered in April 1952, he declared, "The cold, hard fact is that the state in this situation discriminates against Negro children."[10] Seitz concurred with the "Finding of Fact" of the Kansas case that segregation created inequality. But he also agreed that *Plessy* could be over-turned only by the Supreme Court.

Judge Seitz's next words shocked both sides of the dispute. The state was ordered to admit the plaintiffs to the white schools at once. This was to be a temporary solution until the black schools could be brought up to par. Even so, this was the NAACP's first real victory in the battle to desegregate the nation's elementary and grade schools.

Another Setback

By the time *Davis v. County School Board of Prince Edward County* reached the U.S. District Court in Richmond in February 1952, Virginia's attorneys were well prepared. They had followed the progress of the other cases through the courts and knew their opponents' strategy. For the first time, the NAACP faced opposing testimony to their expert witnesses' data.

Attorneys Oliver Hill, Spottswood Robinson, and Robert Carter made the standard arguments of inequality in the school systems. Justin Moore, for the defense, agreed that the schools were unequal. But he declared that the state was currently correcting the problem.

Next, the plaintiffs' lawyers had their experts testify that segregation is harmful to students. Virginia had its own lineup of expert witnesses. The state's lawyers pointed out that the plaintiffs' experts were stating their opinions, not reporting facts. Moore referred to previous opinions written by all three judges of the court upholding the "separate but equal" doctrine in education. In closing remarks, Virginia's attorney general predicted that the people in his state would neither integrate their schools nor would they disobey a court order to desegregate. They would simply shut down all public schools.

The court took only a week to decide against the plaintiffs. They found Virginia to be acting in good faith to make the schools equal. Segregated schooling was a long-established custom and harmed no one, they said. This was the NAACP's most crushing blow. Its hopes were riding on the U.S. Supreme Court now. It did not have long to wait.

CHAPTER FOUR

A Case for Equality

We conclude that in the field of public education the doctrine of "separate but equal" has no place. Separate educational facilities are inherently unequal.[1]

— **Chief Justice Earl Warren**

The Supreme Court had undergone many changes since it had set the future course for American blacks in *Plessy* in 1896. Traditionally, the justices saw their job as a balance to the executive and legislative branches of government. It was the Court's job to see that changes supported by the president or Congress did not conflict with the Constitution.

As Roosevelt's New Deal laws were enacted in the 1930s and 1940s, this narrow view of the Court's role began to interfere with the relief measures the nation needed to recover from the Depression. Time after time, the Court struck down new laws it believed intruded on states' rights. Roosevelt responded by introducing a law to add members to the Supreme Court. That way he could choose justices more sympathetic to his policies. This "court-packing" scheme was defeated, but the message was clear.

As justices retired, Roosevelt and Truman appointed their own men to the

From left, lawyers George E. C. Hayes, Thurgood Marshall, and James M. Nabrit, Jr., congratulate one another May 17, 1954, after the Supreme Court ruled that schools must be desegregated.

43

bench. By the time Fred M. Vinson became chief justice in 1946, the entire Court had been named by Democratic administrations. The justices were not of one mind, though. Vinson had been appointed as a peacemaker, to heal the widening divisions in the Court. Unfortunately, he was ineffective in this role.

In the year before the *Brown* hearing, the Court issued unanimous decisions only 19 percent of the time. When a federal court issues an opinion, any justice is free to attach a dissent, disagreeing with the opinion. Or a justice may add a concurrence, agreeing with the decision but differing in the reasoning behind it. A simple majority carries the full weight of the law. However, in cases where there is public controversy, a divided court sends mixed signals.

Vinson led Associate Justices Harold H. Burton, Stanley F. Reed, Sherman Minton, and Tom C. Clark in the progovernment wing of the court. The early 1950s was a time of increasing tension as the cold war with the Soviet Union escalated. Widespread anticommunist sentiment and concern over spies led to laws favoring national security over personal freedom. Vinson's bloc generally supported federal interests in these cases.

Opposing the conservatives were Hugo L. Black and William O. Douglas, to whom civil liberties were a prime concern. Taking up the centrist position were Felix Frankfurter and Robert H. Jackson. They were known as supporters of judicial restraint. They believed the courts should not indulge in "judicial legislation," which occurs when a court creates a new law by its ruling. Normally, Congress is the branch of government that makes the laws.

Most cases to reach the Supreme Court do so by a writ of certiorari. In order for a case to be heard, at least four justices must vote that it merits a hearing. Then the justices order the certified records of the last court to hear the case be forwarded to them. In a year, the justices receive thousands of petitions for certiorari. They hear only a small fraction of those.

In some instances, the justices believe there are no substantial questions of federal or constitutional law involved. Other times, they believe the issue has already been settled by a prior Supreme Court decision. Only in extreme circumstances will the Court reverse an earlier decision. Once in a while the Court will refuse to hear cases that the justices believe are political in nature.

On the Road to the Supreme Court

The Court had known for some time that the issue of segregation in public elementary and secondary schools would eventually come before it. In June 1952, the justices voted to schedule arguments in the *Brown* and *Briggs* cases for late October of the coming term. Fearing political fallout from the controversial issue, they postponed the hearing until December, after the presidential elections. In the meantime, they added the *Davis* case and requested Nabrit to file a request to hear *Bolling*. Delaware had recently appealed Judge Seitz's order in the *Belton* case to integrate schools in that state. *Belton* was added at the last moment.

The Justice Department was invited to file a brief to present the administration's position. Justice Clark explained later, "We felt it was much better to have representative cases from different parts of the country, and so we consolidated them and made *Brown* the first so that the whole question would not smack of being a purely southern one."[2]

Arguments began on December 9, 1952, and lasted three days. "Oyez! oyez! oyez!" the Court crier intoned as the black-robed justices filed to their places on the bench. Busts of great philosophers looked down on the proceedings from the marble friezes circling the room.

Robert Carter, representing Brown, took his place at the lectern directly below the chief justice. Attorneys for each side had a maximum of one hour to present their cases before the court, less if they wished to reserve time for rebuttal. Carter wasted no time in getting to the heart of the matter. "Here we

The courtroom of the U.S. Supreme Court. This is where the lawyers argue their cases before the justices. The justices enter through the velvet curtains and sit behind the bench. The clock hanging from the ceiling reminds lawyers how much time they have left for their arguments.

abandon any claim . . . of any constitutional inequality which comes from anything other than the act of segregation itself,"[3] he said.

Carter argued that segregation itself harmed his client. It also denied black students "equal protection of the laws" as guaranteed under the Fourteenth Amendment. He said that the decisions of the Court in *Sweatt* and *McLaurin* logically had to extend to public schools as well. He declared there was more to education than what students read in books. He introduced the "Finding of Fact" from the Kansas decision. The research data was presented, supported by the signatures of 35 prominent social scientists.

Paul Wilson, defending Kansas, replied that the *Sweatt* and *McLaurin* cases did not prove that segregation inevitably caused inequality. The state, he argued, could not control the psychological aspects of education. Furthermore, the specific plaintiffs in this case had demonstrated no psychological harm, he said. He invoked *Plessy v. Ferguson* as the precedent for segregation.

Justice Burton indicated where his sympathies lay. He asked if Wilson realized that changes in society in the 56 years since *Plessy* might have rendered that decision invalid.

A Plea for Desegregation

Thurgood Marshall was up next for the *Briggs* case. He bolstered Carter's contention that segregation was harmful without a rational reason for its existence. To counter the argument that this was a matter for state legislatures, he pointed out that the Civil War had been fought to prevent unjust state laws. Marshall said he was not asking the court to dictate local policy. He was asking only that state-mandated segregation be struck down.

Frankfurter objected that such a ruling would surely result in gerrymandering and similar acts. Marshall replied that such problems could be dealt with as they arose. The important thing, he said, was to stop classing people by race.

Then, he said, local districts could take time to work out the details of desegregation. Optimistically, he added, "It might take six months to do it one place and two months to do it another place."[4]

Marshall's opponent, John W. Davis, was the most esteemed constitutional lawyer in the country. He based South Carolina's case on three points: The state had complied with the lower court's order and was working to make its facilities equal. It was clear that the Fourteenth Amendment did not bar classing people by race. And the research presented by Marshall had nothing to do with constitutionally guaranteed rights. He appealed to the justices to preserve states' rights. Surely, of all issues best left to local self-government, he argued, the education of the young was the matter closest to the citizens' hearts.

In rebuttal, Marshall said the Constitution was designed to ensure that the rights of minorities could not be trampled upon by the majority. Justice Reed asked if the disadvantages of a minority should be weighed against the need for law and order. Marshall pointed out that whites were the ones doing the weighing. There were no black legislators in any of the states before the Court.

Glaring Inequalities

The *Davis* case was presented by Spottswood Robinson. He noted the glaring inequalities in Prince Edward County and demanded desegregation at once.

Justin Moore, arguing the case for Virginia, blamed the lack of action on the student strike. He maintained that negative publicity had blocked passage of a bond issue for new schools. Virginia's history and customs, he said, supported the state's right to segregate its schools. Segregation was intended only to improve education for both races, Moore argued. He claimed there was nothing in the Fourteenth Amendment authorizing the court to set local policy. Only another constitutional amendment could change matters, Moore said.

In rebuttal, Robinson claimed Virginia had other, less kindly reasons for segregation. He noted that a leader of Virginia's constitutional convention had promoted school segregation as a way to limit the power of blacks. The Supreme Court, Robinson argued, had already widened its interpretation of the Fourteenth Amendment in other cases without protest.

Washington as a Showpiece

James Nabrit, Jr., and George E. C. Hayes shared duties on the *Bolling* case. Their biggest problem was explaining how their clients' rights had been denied when Congress itself had run separate schools for blacks and whites in the nation's capital for almost a century. They pointed out that the law did not require that schools be segregated. The system, they said, was set up that way because of politics.

Individual rights, the lawyers argued, were not a matter of legislation. The Bill of Rights was a clear reminder of that, they said. Finally, they reminded the court that Washington, D.C., was the nation's showpiece. International relations, particularly with the "colored" peoples of Africa and Asia, were at stake, they warned.

Milton Korman took the floor for Washington. He claimed that Congress never intended to mix the races. Its only desire was to help the newly freed slaves. Korman blundered when he quoted a previous Supreme Court decision that said public opinion should not be used as a basis for laws. His source was the Court's words in the *Dred Scott* case, the decision that led to the Civil War. *Dred Scott* was overturned by the Thirteenth, Fourteenth, and Fifteenth amendments.

Integration Working

Last up was Delaware Attorney General Albert Young. He complained

Thurgood Marshall, right, confers with attorney Spottswood W. Robinson regarding their case to end segregation in the schools.

that Judge Seitz's action in ordering immediate desegregation in the *Belton* case was unnecessary. The state was taking prompt action in making the schools equal.

Arguing for Belton, Louis Redding and Jack Greenberg said that regardless of the improvements to the schools, the Claymont students still had to endure a long bus ride every day. They noted that the schools had already been integrated under Seitz's order, and the two races were getting along with no problems. They asked that the arrangement be made permanent.

Deliberating the Cases

The Court adjourned, and the nation held its breath waiting for the justices' decision. America would have to wait almost a year and a half for their answer. The Saturday following the arguments the justices gathered in the conference room behind the court chamber. Bookcases filled with records of all federal court cases surrounded the long felt-lined table where they sat. No one intruded on their deliberations.

Each justice in turn gave his opinion of the cases. The chief spoke first, then the rest in descending order of seniority. Vinson was not ready to support desegregation. Congress had not outlawed it. Even Justice Harlan had not mentioned schools in his eloquent dissent to *Plessy*. The consequences could be serious, given the mood in the South. He preferred to wait and see the outcome of programs designed to make black and white schools equal.

Black had always been an outspoken champion of individual rights. He believed the purpose of the Civil War amendments was to stop all discrimination due to race. Black grew up in Alabama. As a southerner, he had no illusions as to the purpose of segregation. He knew what troubles lay ahead but thought desegregating the schools was the right thing to do.

Reed disagreed with Black. Segregation did not equal discrimination in his eyes. Reed did not think Virginia would accept desegregation for at least ten years. He also favored giving the equal schools programs a chance to work.

Felix Frankfurter spoke next. He was sympathetic to the blacks' fight for justice. Frankfurter was Jewish and had felt the sting of discrimination before. But he was also a strong believer in the stability of the law. To change the long-standing customs of 21 states would require massive federal intervention. The Court should not make rulings it could not enforce, he argued. If the justices did order desegregation, Frankfurter noted, it would be important how it was presented. If the Court drew a line in the sand, he said, the South would surely step over it. Frankfurter suggested that the attorneys argue the case again. That would allow time to see how the equal schools programs went. The incoming Eisenhower administration would also have time to express its views. After all, the executive branch would have to enforce any action required.

William Douglas's vote was never in doubt. He saw the Court as a way to balance power—a last chance to prevent abuses by the other two branches of the government. He urged an end to segregation.

Jackson suggested a more cautious route. He worried that overturning such a long-standing law would be a dangerous precedent. He did not think there was a judicial reason to strike down *Plessy*. Even though he believed desegregation was inevitable and desirable, he knew it would not cure racism. He suggested not voting that day, but discussing the case over the next few months.

Burton was ready to vote for the plaintiffs. Though quite conservative, he was aware of his moral duty. Times had changed since the Reconstruction, he noted. The system of separate schools that had been set up to help blacks learn was now hindering them.

Clark, on the other hand, was not prepared to take a position yet. He wanted to delay the decision.

Sherman Minton, the junior member of the court, argued that *Sweatt* and *McLaurin* could be cited as precedents to overturn *Plessy*. He believed segregation was unreasonable and unconstitutional.

Warren Joins the Court

The Court waited until June 1953 to make a decision—which was not to decide the case yet. Frankfurter had convinced the others that the case should be argued again. The attorneys for both sides were told to prepare for a hearing the following October. They were to answer five questions:

1. Had the men who framed and ratified the Fourteenth Amendment intended to abolish segregated schools?
2. How did they intend for future Congresses to handle the issue?
3. Did the amendment allow the Court to end segregation?
4. Could the Court allow a gradual transition?
5. What sort of decree should the Court make?

The Justice Department was requested to submit a new brief and join in the oral arguments this time. Both sides went to work, searching history and law books for answers to the Court's questions. That summer, however, something happened that would bring a profound change to the Court.

In September, as the Court prepared for a new term, Chief Justice Vinson died of a heart attack. President Dwight Eisenhower appointed Earl Warren, governor of California, to fill his seat. Eisenhower was aware of the political consequences of the upcoming *Brown* decision. He favored desegregation, but only as a gradual process. He did not want to upset southern voters, who had shown unexpected support for the Republican candidate.

Warren was known as being honest and fair during his years as California attorney general. As governor during World War II, he had urged that Japanese Americans be placed in camps to protect national security. The president believed Warren would favor a law-and-order court and avoid controversial decisions.

Warren was soon accepted by the associate justices as a natural leader. He was a dedicated worker and tried hard to bring the splintered Court together. No one knew how he would vote on *Brown*.

In December 1953, Warren joined his peers on the Court to hear the *Brown* arguments. Neither side came up with convincing arguments about what the Reconstruction Congress had intended when it wrote the Fourteenth Amendment. Public education was rare at the time it was written, and little mention was made of it. However, the Reconstruction Congress had set up segregated schools in Washington, D.C.

The attorneys against segregation once again argued that excluding black children from white schools violated the equal protection clause of the Fourteenth Amendment. Their clients, they said, were not being treated equally under the law.

The NAACP's position was that the amendment was meant to ban all discrimination. Thurgood Marshall argued that the only way for his opponents to win would be to prove that the terms of the Fourteenth Amendment specifically excluded schools. James Nabrit, Jr., drew a parallel to George Orwell's *Animal Farm*, with its satirical commandment, "All animals are equal, but some animals are more equal than others."[5] John Davis, in his turn, pleaded for states' rights. He warned the Court that it could not act "as a glorified board of education."[6]

The argument of Assistant Attorney General J. Lee Rankin, speaking for the Justice Department, was perhaps the most telling. The administration stuck

Chief Justice Earl Warren in a photograph taken in 1962

Members of the Supreme Court pose for their official portrait, May 23, 1955. From left, seated: Felix Frankfurter, Hugo Black, Chief Justice Earl Warren, Stanley Reed, William O. Douglas; standing: Sherman Minton, Harold H. Burton, Tom Clark, and John M. Harlan. Harlan joined the court in 1955 after the death of Robert Jackson.

by its original brief that segregation should be stopped. Education may not have been a constitutionally guaranteed right, Rankin argued. But once the states required students to attend school, he said, they had to offer equal education to all. Segregated facilities could not be equal, Rankin said. He suggested letting the lower courts oversee the ruling by giving the states no more than a year to present plans to desegregate the schools.

Warren spoke first at the justices' Saturday morning conference following the arguments. He said that he regretted overturning a precedent but that segregation could no longer be justified. He noted that the Court must agree on such an important decision.

As Warren put it:

> You know, we don't have money at the court for an army, and we can't take ads in the newspapers, and we don't want to go out on a picket-line in our robes. We have to convince the nation by the force of our opinions.[7]

Despite Warren's arguments, none of the associate justices changed their minds. They agreed not to vote until they had discussed the issue further.

Over the next few months, Warren proved his skill as peacemaker. Noting that some feared chaos if the Court simply declared segregation illegal, Warren said clear guidelines were needed. He also noted that local feelings must be taken into account when setting up desegregation plans.

Soon, only Reed balked at ordering desegregation. As a southerner, Reed would weaken the Court's position considerably if he dissented. His main concern was the racial unrest that would doubtless follow the Court's order. Extracting a promise from Warren to go slow on setting up desegregation plans, he finally agreed to go along with the rest.

After a Century, Injustice Falls

On May 17, 1954, Chief Justice Earl Warren read the unanimous opinion of the Court. As reporters and the nation listened, he told of the history of the cases and the importance of education to the nation. He quoted the Kansas "Finding of Fact" on the psychological effect of segregation. Then he spoke the words that were to echo through every schoolroom in the country:

We come then to the question presented: Does segregation of children in public schools solely on the basis of race, even though the physical facilities and other "tangible" factors may be equal, deprive the children of the minority group of equal educational opportunities? We believe that it does.[8]

The cases were to be argued once again in the next term to plan how the ruling would be enforced. The best way to desegregate the schools would be worked out then. Attorneys general of all segregating states were invited to participate.

Justice Reed, the last holdout, felt tears streaming down his face as he watched the injustice of a century fall before the words of the Court. After his retirement, he stated that *Brown* was the most important case he ever decided. But he feared for the future. How would the South accept the change? Only time would tell—and as it turned out, it was a long time indeed.

Black and white students eat their lunches side by side at the Ninde S. Wilder Elementary School in Louisville, Kentucky, after the U.S. Supreme Court ordered the schools to integrate. There were no disturbances. Twenty-six black students were among the 660 students enrolled in the school.

Troops stand ready to protect black students attending Central High School in Little Rock, Arkansas, in 1957. Earlier, Governor Orval Faubus had ordered the National Guard to surround the school to prevent desegregation.

From Brown to Green

*You cannot change people's hearts
merely by laws.*[1]

— Dwight D. Eisenhower

Immediate reaction to the decision was muted. The Court's judgment was somewhat less than what the NAACP lawyers had hoped. With no timetable in place, they feared the plaintiffs would be out of school by the time any real changes took place. Black people were hopeful, but wary. They had heard promises many times before.

The southern states remained quiet. There was nothing definite yet to complain about. Even so, the threat of future trouble hung in the air. Within five weeks of the decision, the governor of Virginia announced, "I shall use every legal means at my command to continue segregated schools in Virginia."[2]

Arguments on how to implement the decision were scheduled after the November elections. Justice Robert Jackson died before *Brown* came before the Court a third time. President Eisenhower appointed John Marshall Harlan, grandson and namesake of the *Plessy* dissenter, to take his place. Segregationists regarded the appointment as a slap in the face. Southern senators held up

61

Young black students walk with white schoolmates after attending classes at the Milford, Delaware, high school in September 1954. A short time later the president of the school board announced that all 11 black students attending the newly integrated school had been dropped from the school's rolls.

Harlan's confirmation until March 1955. Warren delayed action on *Brown* until he had a full Court.

In the meantime, some efforts to integrate schools were already under way. Topeka's school board had decided to change its policy before the second Supreme Court hearing. In most places, desegregation went smoothly. Washington, D.C., Louisville, Baltimore, and St. Louis began integrating with few problems. Spottswood Bolling's school was integrated before he graduated.

The first signs of resistance came from Milford, Delaware. The Delaware State Board of Education had directed local school districts to submit desegregation plans to comply with the Supreme Court ruling. The Milford School Board proceeded on its own. Eleven black students were ordered admitted to the tenth grade of the formerly all-white Lakeview Avenue School. Although the white students accepted the new arrangements, parents and other adults picketed outside.

The school board appealed to state authorities to back up its decision to integrate the schools. Instead, the state board refused to issue a ruling. The board claimed that Milford officials had exceeded their authority by not clearing their decision with the state board first. The board did concede that it would have been illegal to refuse to admit the black students. Faced with no state support and threats of violence from the protestors, the members of the Milford School Board resigned.

The state board assumed control of Milford's schools. The high school was closed for a week. When it reopened, the black students attended classes under police guard. Parents kept most of the white students out of school. The demonstrations continued outside the school, and protests spread to other nearby towns. A cross was burned in the field across from the high school. Mothers sent their young children to march in the street carrying signs with anti-integration slogans.

After several more days of growing protests, the segregationists won the battle. Milford's new school board, once more in control, announced that the black students were being removed from the school. They were sent to the all-black school, 20 miles away. The black pupils' parents immediately filed suit to reinstate their children in the white school. As the case slowly made its way through the courts, the black students' rights were upheld. Court orders prevented them from returning to Lakeview Avenue School, though, until the appeal process was completed.

It soon became clear that implementing the Supreme Court's order on the local level was going to be difficult. Further directives from the Court were needed. Many local and state officials didn't want to accept the responsibility for desegregation themselves. Milford's troubles were not unique. By the time the Supreme Court heard rearguments in April, half the counties in the Deep South states had voted to stop desegregation at all costs.

Privately, the NAACP had agreed to accept gradual change as a compromise. The cooperation of the southern states was essential. In Court, though, the NAACP lawyers asked for immediate desegregation. At the very least, they argued, the Court should set a firm date. Thurgood Marshall believed that threats of resistance and even violence were overblown. He noted that similar threats had accompanied the court-ordered restoration of black voting rights but nothing had come of them.

The states, however, were defiant. They threatened to cut off funding for schools and to repeal laws that required students to attend school. South Carolina asked that local courts oversee the schools, since conditions varied from one state to the next. Florida asked for a grace period. Texas leaders were more blunt. They said it was their problem and demanded that the Court let them handle it.

Marshall pointed out that Florida had resisted admitting blacks to the state

Black leaders attend a planning session arranged by the NAACP in Atlanta, Georgia, in June 1955. The leaders were discussing the latest Supreme Court ruling on school desegregation. Thurgood Marshall is second from the left.

law school for five years. There was no reason to believe that under local control the state would do any better. Furthermore, it was not right to adopt different plans for different areas, Marshall said. The rest of the Constitution was administered in the same way all over the country. Why, he asked, should the Fourteenth Amendment be any different?

The Justice Department argued against any deadline. But it said the Court should insist that desegregation programs begin immediately. Desegregation in the armed forces had shown there was the least friction when change happened all at once and enforcement was uniform and firm.

Warren supported the Justice Department's position. No deadline should be set, he said, as long as progress was being made. Lower courts should be given guidelines and allowed to handle local cases as they saw fit. The other justices agreed. On May 31, 1955, Warren read the Court's unanimous decision.

The states were to begin desegregation plans immediately. There was no timetable, but they were ordered to proceed "with all deliberate speed."[3] This phrase proved to be key to the decision. It was meant to encourage states to act without forcing them to finish their plans within a set amount of time. Warren worded the decision that way to ensure that the full Court would agree to the ruling. He also hoped the lack of a timetable would prevent states from defying a Supreme Court order. Justice would be served, but at a pace the South could live with—or so he thought.

Enforcing the Order

Their victory in the schools encouraged blacks to fight for desegregation in other areas. Although the Court had taken the heart out of *Plessy*, it was left to Rosa Parks to bury it. Like many other southern cities, Montgomery, Alabama, required blacks to sit in the back of city buses. Parks, tired after a hard day at work as a maid, sat in the front of the black section. The bus driver

The Reverend Martin Luther King, Jr., speaks to a crowded room of supporters at the Holt Street Baptist Church in Montgomery, Alabama, on March 22, 1956. King urged his listeners to support the bus boycott in the city to protest discrimination against blacks.

67

ordered her to move to make room for white passengers. A Montgomery law required blacks to move for whites, even if the blacks were sitting in the black section. Parks, however, refused to move. Within six months of the *Brown* decision, Parks and a Montgomery pastor, Martin Luther King, Jr., had sparked a citywide boycott of the bus system. It went on for more than a year. Finally, the Supreme Court declared segregation on public transportation illegal. *Plessy* had at last been fully overturned.

The effectiveness of the boycott encouraged other blacks, many of them high-school students. Soon blacks held sit-ins at white-only lunch counters. They went on "freedom rides" on buses in the South to test segregation laws. By 1956, beaches in Baltimore and a golf course in Atlanta were open to blacks. Michigan and Missouri ended segregation in municipal housing. In 1957, Congress passed the first civil rights bill to protect voting rights since the Reconstruction.

Over the next dozen years, the Warren Court opened more doors for minorities. Parks, restaurants, hotels, libraries, and courtrooms were desegregated. A candidate's race could no longer be listed on ballots. Interracial marriage was no longer a crime.

As the barriers fell, there was relatively little protest, once the law was clear. Only with school desegregation was there massive resistance. After two years of efforts to integrate the schools, not one black child attended a white school in Alabama, Florida, Georgia, Louisiana, Mississippi, North and South Carolina, or Virginia.

The southern states used a number of techniques to get around the *Brown* ruling. Many school districts adopted "freedom of choice" policies. Pupils were free to go to whatever school in the district they wanted—if there was room. Officials made sure that white schools were always filled to capacity.

Pupil-placement laws were designed to make changing schools difficult. If

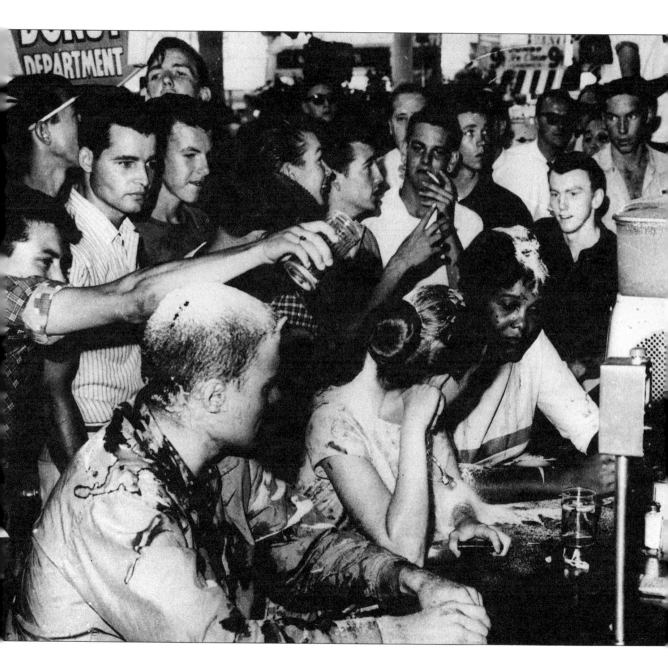

Whites pour sugar, ketchup, and mustard on demonstrators participating in a sit-in at a lunch counter in Jackson, Mississippi. The demonstrators were protesting the restaurant's policy of not allowing blacks to eat there.

69

students wanted to change their schools, they were required to complete a battery of tests and forms. If they failed, it was up to the students to prove they were being discriminated against. Local courts told those who filed suits to take their complaints to local government offices first. The red tape was too much to bother with for most. Even integrated schools often had only a few token blacks.

Violent demonstrations greeted some black children. In Charlotte, the first black girl to break the color barrier at a formerly all-white school reported, "I started walking toward the school, a lot of people were just pushing and shoving and calling me names and throwing things, spitting on me and saying . . . 'Nigger go back to Africa.'"[4]

Throughout it all, the blacks stood alone. Congress was in the hands of Dixiecrats, southern Democrats who did not want to anger their supporters. The Eisenhower administration looked the other way. Federal court orders to desegregate in Alabama and Texas were ignored, and no action was taken.

Not until 1957 did the president reluctantly step in. Governor Orval Faubus ordered the National Guard to surround Central High School in Little Rock, Arkansas, to prevent desegregation. This was too flagrant a violation of federal law. Eisenhower sent in paratroopers to reassert federal authority. But he still did not speak out for desegregation.

It was not until John F. Kennedy became president in 1961 that blacks had a friend in the White House again.

Kennedy Steps In

Kennedy stepped up the hiring of blacks in federal departments. He directed the Interstate Commerce Commission to enforce desegregation at bus and train stations. U.S. marshals were assigned to protect freedom riders. In 1962, Kennedy sent troops to Mississippi to safeguard James Meredith, the lone black student entering the state university.

Dorothy Counts, 15, the first black student to attend Harding High School in Charlotte, North Carolina, endures the taunts of white students on her way to school. A family friend, Dr. Edwin Tompkins, escorted her. Dorothy said she had expected the jeering but hoped it would stop soon.

The year 1963 marked a turning point in the battle. In April, the Reverend Martin Luther King, Jr., led a series of marches in Birmingham, Alabama, to protest discrimination. The marchers were nonviolent, but local police arrested them by the hundreds. Pictures of women and children being attacked by dogs and fire hoses were broadcast to the world on the nightly news.

The president was embarrassed. When Governor George Wallace deployed the National Guard, defying a court order to admit blacks to the University of Alabama, Kennedy had had enough. He put the guard under federal control. Then he appeared on television to appeal for cooperation.

"We must recognize that segregation in education—and I mean de facto segregation in the North as well as the proclaimed segregation in the South—brings with it serious handicaps to a large population,"[5] he said.

A week later, the president sent Congress a proposal that would become the Civil Rights Act of 1964. It provided relief for minorities in many areas. Federal funds were forbidden to go to any state program that was discriminatory. All public accommodations were ordered desegregated. The attorney general was directed to sue on behalf of victims of discrimination in schools and public facilities.

Demonstrators marched in Washington, D.C., and New York City to protest discrimination. They were joined by the Reverend King and Malcolm X, a rising champion of black rights. Black nationalism began to spread.

In the wake of Kennedy's assassination, in November 1963, President Lyndon Baines Johnson pushed the new Civil Rights bill through Congress. Over the next decade, the Justice Department brought suit against 500 school districts for discrimination. The Department of Health, Education, and Welfare (HEW) took 600 such actions.

In January 1964, the Twenty-fourth Amendment, banning poll taxes, was ratified.

Thousands gather around the Washington Monument on August 28, 1963, during the March on Washington to protest discrimination.

Case Returns to Haunt Court

Ten years after *Brown* was decided, the Supreme Court reviewed the progress of desegregation when one of the five cases returned to haunt them. In Prince Edward County, public schools had been closed in 1959 and white students were issued vouchers to enter private schools. Barbara Johns was horrified. Concerned for her safety, her parents had sent Barbara away to finish her senior year. Now she was chagrined at what she had started. At least before the case, the blacks had received some education. Finally, they were to receive some real help.

The border states had done relatively well in desegregating their schools. More than 55 percent of black children in those states now attended integrated schools. But in the states of the old Confederacy, that figure was barely more than 1 percent. In Mississippi, not one black went to school with whites. Clearly something needed to be done.

On May 25, 1964, the Supreme Court signaled a shifting of gears. Justice Black, writing for the Court, said, "The time for mere 'deliberate speed' has run out, and that phrase can no longer justify denying these Prince Edward County schoolchildren their constitutional rights to an education equal to that afforded by the public schools in other parts of Virginia."[6] The decision required the county to raise money from taxes to operate public schools.

By now, black voter registration campaigns were having the desired effect. There were twice as many black voters as three years before. Candidates for Congress and the Senate began to seek the black vote. In 1965, the Voting Rights Act was passed after enormous rallies were held in Selma, Alabama. The 1964 murder of three civil rights workers—two whites from the North and a black from Mississippi—had spurred rapid passage.

Several advances were made in the next few years. The federal government began to subsidize local schools. This aid provided another fiscal weapon

Hundreds of schoolchildren listen to the Reverend James Bevel of Atlanta during a
school boycott in 1964 protesting segregation in Boston schools.

Black schoolchildren are led to an old armory after their arrest for demonstrating in front of the county courthouse in Selma, Alabama, on February 4, 1965. The demonstration was part of a mass voter-registration drive.

to fight discrimination. The courts ordered school boards to include teachers in their desegregation plans. Up to now, integrating schools often meant moving black students to white schools and firing most of the black teachers.

The Supreme Court struck down freedom of choice plans in the case of *Green v. County School Board of New Kent County*. New Kent, a rural Virginia county, had adopted a freedom of choice plan in 1965, but in three years 85 percent of black students still attended all-black schools. The Court ruled that the system was illegal and ordered school boards to integrate their schools and eliminate discrimination "root and branch."[7]

*S*wann and *B*eyond

*[We] must eventually surrender race
solidarity and the idea of American
Negro culture to the concept of world
humanity, above race and nation. This is
the price of liberty. This is the cost of
oppression.*[1]

— W. E. B. DuBois

As the 1960s drew to a close, American blacks could
look back on a decade of breakthroughs. The 1968 Fair Housing Act helped to
end some discrimination in private sales of homes. Robert Weaver was the first
black ever appointed to a Cabinet post. Massachusetts voters elected Edward
Brooke as the first black senator since the Reconstruction. In 1967, President
Johnson selected Thurgood Marshall as the first black to sit on the Supreme
Court. Blacks were becoming a part of the popular culture as entertainers such
as Bill Cosby appeared on television shows.

Yet things grew worse in other areas. As suburban regions grew, blacks
were increasingly concentrated in inner-city ghettos. The Vietnam War sapped

**President Lyndon B. Johnson, left, congratulates Thurgood Marshall in 1967 after the
president announced he was nominating Marshall to serve on the Supreme Court.
Marshall was the first black to serve on the High Court.**

the nation's resources. The Justice Department, busy with street crime cases, prosecuted fewer discrimination violators. Richard M. Nixon was elected president on a law-and-order platform. Courting the southern states, he ordered a slowdown of desegregation efforts.

In 1969, a Mississippi school board asked for a delay of several months in adopting a desegregation plan. Local blacks protested. The case, *Alexander v. Holmes County Board of Education*, rapidly reached the Supreme Court.

Justice Black, writing for the Court, said the schools had made only a "glacial movement"[2] toward desegregation. Stubborn school boards were ordered to "begin immediately to operate as unitary school systems."[3]

Robert Finch, the head of HEW, directed Mississippi to desegregate. President Nixon, pressured by southern politicians, told Finch to ignore the Supreme Court and delay the order. Finch and his top aides resigned in protest. Federal judges carried through on the Court order, and the southern states complied.

The effect of the order was immediate. In the year following the ruling, black enrollment in integrated schools increased from 10 percent to 90 percent. There was little violence. By now, most people knew that desegregation was inevitable. One barrier remained to completing the task of integrating the nation's schools.

Equal Schools for the Poor

In many communities, blacks and whites lived in separate parts of town. School segregation resulted because students attended schools closest to their homes. Black neighborhoods were generally less wealthy than white ones so less money was available for schools. The problem became worse as those who could moved to communities with better schools. The result was lowered property values. Poorer people then moved into the area and fed the vicious cycle.

Richard M. Nixon signals victory as he makes his acceptance speech after being nominated as the Republican presidential candidate in 1968.

Parents did not want their children attending poorer schools. The government could do little to control where people chose to live. But blacks in Charlotte, North Carolina, knew that school districts could be changed.

In 1964, only 2 percent of Charlotte's blacks attended integrated schools. That year, six-year-old James E. Swann was denied admission to a white school near his home. His father had a secure job teaching at Johnson C. Smith University. The NAACP decided that Swann was the best candidate to head a desegregation lawsuit.

Swann v. Charlotte-Mecklenburg Board of Education started the long journey toward the Supreme Court. By September 1968, the suit had reached Federal District Court Judge James B. McMillan. The *Green* case had been decided only recently. McMillan ruled, "The law has moved from an attitude barring discrimination to an attitude requiring active desegregation. The actions of school boards and district courts must now be judged under *Green v. New Kent County* rather than under the milder lash of *Brown v. Board of Education*."[4]

Charlotte was ordered to submit a plan for desegregation. The board could use busing, redistricting, or any other means to accomplish this. However, it had to be effective. The school board made a halfhearted attempt to devise a plan. McMillan ruled it unacceptable. A court-appointed expert was asked to come up with a workable scheme.

Dr. John A. Finger believed busing to be the only answer. The Finger Plan called for each black inner-city school to be paired with two or three white schools in outlying areas. Older white students would be bused to the city schools. Younger black students would be bused to the suburbs.

There was an immediate public outcry. White parents would not stand for their children being bused for miles to attend the poorly equipped schools in the city. Judge McMillan was hanged in effigy. Julius LeVonne Chambers, the NAACP lawyer, had his house and car dynamited. In Washington, President Nixon denounced the plan.

Proponents of the Finger Plan pointed out that 60 percent of the students in the state rode buses anyway. In the 1950s, North Carolina proudly had proclaimed itself "the school-busingest state in the Union."[5] The white parents who were championing neighborhood schools had never complained when it was the black students being bused past nearby schools to attend segregated facilities.

One of the most controversial aspects of the Finger Plan was its use of racial quotas. Seventy-one percent of the students in the district were white; 29 percent were black. Dr. Finger suggested aiming for this same ratio in each of the schools. McMillan decided not to require exact quotas. The ratio would be used only as a rough guideline.

Swann appeared before the Supreme Court in October 1970. Attorney Chambers, presenting his first case before the Court, asked the justices whether a school board could continue segregation when a plan to desegregate existed.

Justice Black grilled him from the bench. "Is there a constitutional requirement to bus pupils and to force states to buy a large number of buses?"[6] he asked. "The Constitution allows it,"[7] was the answer.

Black pressed his point. Was it essential? he asked. Chambers did not back down. He replied, "The Constitution requires whatever is necessary to desegregate."[8]

In conference, Black hesitated to extend the Court's constitutional powers. "Where does the word *busing* appear in the Constitution?"[9] he wanted to know. The new chief justice, Warren Earl Burger, was also doubtful. Thurgood Marshall was, of course, determined to carry on the battle now that he was an associate justice. Douglas and Brennan also supported the plaintiff's position. John Marshall Harlan had assumed Frankfurter's former role as the voice of judicial restraint. Potter Stewart often joined him in a centrist position. The conservative wing consisted of Harry Blackmun and Byron White.

The 1964 Civil Rights Act had been quite specific on the issue of busing. The bill read, "Nothing herein shall empower any official or court of the United States to issue any order seeking to achieve a racial balance in any school by

The Supreme Court justices pose for an official portrait in 1971. Seated, from left: John M. Harlan, Hugo L. Black, Chief Justice Warren E. Burger, William O. Douglas, and William J. Brennan, Jr. Standing, from left: Thurgood Marshall, Potter Stewart, Byron R. White, and Harry A. Blackmun.

requiring the transportation of pupils or students from one school to another."[10] But nothing forbade them to do so, Douglas noted. The intention of the passage was to make it clear that Congress was granting no new authority to the Court. The Court's authority in such cases lay in the Fourteenth Amendment. And that authority required the Court to fix situations that violated the Constitution.

Chief Justice Burger announced the Court's decision in *Swann* in April 1971. The decision was once again unanimous. Neighborhood schools were certainly the preferred school system, everything else being equal, according to the Court. "But all things are not equal in a system that has been deliberately constructed and maintained to enforce racial segregation,"[11] Burger read. The Finger Plan was upheld.

The decision discussed how neighborhoods tended to develop around schools. Communities would not be allowed to build schools in areas that encouraged segregation. Freedom of choice plans were only permissible if transportation was free. Room had to be provided at the schools for new students. Quotas were acceptable only as a starting point to determine if there was a problem.

There was an immediate protest across the nation. President Nixon directed the Justice Department to draft a constitutional amendment against busing. But the southern states complied with the decision. Within two years, more than 46 percent of the black students in the Deep South states attended schools with a majority of whites. By comparison, only 28 percent of the blacks in the North and West went to such schools.

The battle for justice moved out of the South into the northern cities. Boston, Denver, and Detroit became embroiled in their own court cases over school segregation. The problems of poor, mostly black ghetto schools remain unresolved today.

The Battle Continues

Efforts to desegregate the schools have met with successes and failures. By 1974 more than 13 times as many blacks were registered to vote in Mississippi as 10 years before. Jackson, Mississippi, swimming pools were finally integrated. Linda Brown was a grown woman with two children who attended a long-integrated school. Robert Carter was a U.S. District Court Judge. Spottswood Robinson sat on the Court of Appeals in Washington.

Other areas still needed improvement. Washington and Wilmington schools were 90 percent black. In Summerton, South Carolina, 20 years after *Brown*, 3,000 blacks went to school with a single white student.

Desegregation efforts continue today. Every year brings fresh court cases in American cities. Schools change as the national economy shifts and people move to new areas.

The strength of constitutional law is twofold. The solid base of past cases prevents the same battles from being fought over and over again. And, because it is flexible, the law can adapt to changing times. Sometimes the wheels of justice turn slowly, but there is always hope for progress.

In most places, minorities are far better off than they were when Linda Brown walked those few blocks to the white school with her father. Charlotte is one city where desegregation has worked. After a testimonial dinner for Judge McMillan and attorney Chambers in 1981, the *Charlotte Observer* noted as much.

Schools are no longer black or white, but are simply schools. As a result, the racial composition of surrounding areas is not as critical as it once was. The center city and its environs are a healthy mixture of black and white neighborhoods.[12]

Police were on hand to protect students as they arrived at the Lewenburg School in the Mattapan section of Boston on September 19, 1974. Some schools reported fighting, and buses were stoned on the sixth day of busing to integrate Boston schools.

Linda Brown Smith, left, listens to Benjamin Hooks, executive director of the NAACP, during ceremonies in Columbia, South Carolina, on May 18, 1979, marking the 25th anniversary of the Supreme Court's school desegregation decision. Smith was the lead plaintiff in the case.

Some cities, though, are worse than ever. Schools in some inner-city slums struggle to provide an adequate education for minority children caught in the morass of poverty and crime.

The fight for racial equality has come at great cost. It has been paid for with human lives offered with great courage and dignity. As the Reverend Joseph DeLaine waited to hear the last Supreme Court *Brown* hearing, his words echoed the heartache and triumph of his efforts. "There were times when I thought I would go out of my mind because of this case," he told a reporter. Then he added, "If I had to do it again, I would. I feel that it was worth it."[13] For millions of schoolchildren in the generations to come, the chance for a decent life made it all worthwhile.

Source **N**otes

Chapter One

1. Richard Kluger, *Simple Justice: The History of Brown v. Board of Education and Black America's Struggle for Racial Equality* (New York: Vintage Books, 1975), p. 71.

2. Ibid., p. 408.

3. Marjorie G. Fribourg, *The Supreme Court in American History: Ten Great Decisions—The People, the Times and the Issues* (Philadelphia: Macrae Smith Company, 1965), p. 132.

4. Kluger, p. 515.

Chapter Two

1. Kluger, p. 82.

2. Don Lawson, *Landmark Supreme Court Cases* (Hillside, New Jersey: Enslow Publishers, 1987), p. 32.

3. Kluger, p. 72.

4. Ibid., p. 74.

5. Fribourg, p. 130.

6. *United States Reports*, vol. 163 (Washington, D.C.: U.S. Government Printing Office, 1896), p. 562.

Chapter Three

1. Kluger, p. 524.

2. Ibid., p. 264.

3. Ibid., p. 282.

4. Arthur S. Link, Robert V. Remini, Douglas Greenberg, and Robert C. McMath, Jr., *A Concise History of the American People* (Arlington Heights, Illinois: Harlan Davidson, 1984), p. A-8.

5. Kluger, pp. 521-522.

6. Ibid., p. 522.

7. Ibid., p. 415.

8. Ibid., p. 424.

9. Ibid.

10. Ibid., p. 449.

Chapter Four

1. *New York Times* (May 18, 1954), p. 15.

2. Kluger, p. 540.

3. Ibid., p. 564.

4. Ibid., p. 572.

5. George Orwell, *Animal Farm* (New York: The New American Library, 1946), p. 123.

6. Kluger, p. 672.

7. Ibid., p. 706.

8. *New York Times* (May 18, 1954), p. 15.

Chapter Five

1. Barbara Habenstreit, *Changing America and the Supreme Court* (New York: Julian Messner, 1970), p. 158.

2. Kluger, p. 714.

3. *New York Times* (June 1, 1955), p. 28.

4. Bernard Schwartz, *Swann's Way: The School Busing Case and the Supreme Court* (New York: Oxford University Press, 1986), p. 8.

5. Meyer Weinberg, *A Chance to Learn: The History of Race and Education in the United States* (New York: Cambridge University Press, 1977), p. 107.

6. Fribourg, p. 142.

7. Schwartz, p. 61.

Chapter Six

1. Weinberg, p. 87.

2. Schwartz, p. 68.

3. Ibid., p. 86.

4. Ibid., p. 15.

5. Ibid., p. 19.

6. Ibid., p. 97.

7. Ibid.

8. Ibid., p. 98.

9. Ibid., p. 35.

10. Ibid., p. 105.

11. Ibid., p. 237.

12. Ibid., p. 191.

13. Kluger, p. 667.

Further **R**eading

Ashmore, Harry S. *The Negro and the Schools*. Chapel Hill: University of North Carolina Press, 1954.

Barrett, Russell H. *Integration at Ole Miss*. Chicago: Quadrangle Books, 1965.

Coy, Harold, (revised by Greenberg, Lorna.) *The Supreme Court*. New York: F. Watts, 1981.

Fenderson, Lewis H. *Thurgood Marshall: Fighter for Justice*. New York: McGraw-Hill, 1969.

Forte, David F. *The Supreme Court*. New York: F. Watts, 1979.

Franklin, John Hope. *From Slavery to Freedom: A History of Negro Americans*, 3rd ed. New York: Alfred A. Knopf, 1967.

Fribourg, Marjorie G. *The Supreme Court in American History: Ten Great Decisions—The People, the Times and the Issues*. Philadelphia: Macrae Smith Company, 1965.

Garraty, John A., ed. *Quarrels That Have Shaped the Constitution*. New York: Harper & Row, 1987.

Goode Stephen. *The Controversial Court: Supreme Court Influences on American Life*. New York: Messner, 1982.

Greene, Carol. *The Supreme Court*. Chicago: Childrens Press, 1985.

Habenstreit, Barbara. *Changing America and the Supreme Court*. New York: Julian Messner, 1970.

King, Martin Luther, Jr. *Stride Toward Freedom: The Montgomery Story*. New York: Harper & Row, 1958.

Kluger, Richard. *Simple Justice: The History of Brown v. Board of Education and Black America's Struggle for Racial Equality*. New York: Vintage Books, 1975.

Lawson, Don. *Landmark Supreme Court Cases*. Hillside, New Jersey: Enslow
    Publishers, 1987.

Lewis, Anthony. *Gideon's Trumpet*. New York: Random House, 1966.

Marquardt, Dorothy A. *A Guide to the Supreme Court*. Indianapolis:
    Bobbs-Merrill, 1977.

Miller, Loren. *The Petitioners: The Story of the Supreme Court of the United
    States and the Negro*. New York: Pantheon Books, 1966.

Muse, Benjamin. *Ten Years of Prelude: The Story of Integration Since the
    Supreme Court's 1954 Decision*. New York: Viking Press, 1964.

Peters, William. *A Class Divided*. Garden City, N.Y.: Doubleday, 1971.

Peterson, Helen Stone. *The Supreme Court in America's Story*. Scarsdale,
    N.Y.: Garrard Publishing Co., 1976.

Schwartz, Bernard. *A Basic History of the U.S. Supreme Court*. Princeton:
    Van Nostrand, 1968.

Stein, R. Conrad. *The Story of the Powers of the Supreme Court*. Chicago:
    Childrens Press, 1989.

Stevens, Leonard. *Equal: The Case of Integration vs. Jim Crow*. New York:
    Coward, McCann & Geoghegan, 1975.

Tresolini, Rocco. *Historic Decisions of the Supreme Court*. Philadelphia: J.B.
    Lippincott, 1963.

Williams, Juan. *Eyes on the Prize: America's Civil Rights Year, 1954-1965*.
    New York: Viking Press, 1987.

Index